THE REAL ESTATE CONNECTOR METHOD

A Quick Start Guide to

Wholesaling Real Estate with Zero

Money, Credit or Experience

The Ligon Brothers

Michael & David Ligon

THE REAL ESTATE CONNECTOR METHOD
& THE LYNK WHOLESALING SYSTEM

ISBN: 9798676233419

CONTENT

Disclaimer

The Ligon Brothers are not CPA's, Realtors® or Attorneys. Any information that is found or derived from this documentation or any product(s), service(s), tactic(s), techniques and/or idea(s) discussed or described, is NOT to be construed as legal, medical, personal or financial advice. The information provided in the documents, videos, materials, products, websites, etc. is not to be interpreted as a guarantee and/or promise of earnings. The earning potential is solely and entirely dependent on the individual using the product(s), service(s), tactic(s), techniques and/or idea(s) discussed or described.

The Ligon Brothers cannot guarantee the success or profit potential of anyone using the product(s), service(s), tactic(s), techniques and/or idea(s) discussed or described. We cannot guarantee your success. Any and all claims made by the Ligon Brothers are to be considered as exceptional by seasoned professionals and not the average result of any person(s) that using the product(s), service(s), tactic(s), techniques and/or idea(s) discussed or described. There are a numerous amount of factors that will play a role in determining your actual results. No guarantees are made that you will achieve the same or similar results as The Ligon Brothers and/or any of their students or examples discussed.

NO GUARANTEES ARE MADE THAT ANYONE
USING THE PRODUCT(S), SERVICE(S),
TACTIC(S), TECHNIQUES AND/OR IDEA(S)
DISCUSSED, DESCRIBED, MENTIONED IN OUR
MATERIAL AND/OR ON OUR WEBSITES,
VIDEO(S) AND SOCIAL MEDIA ACCOUNTS WILL
ACHIEVE ANY RESULTS AT ALL. YOU ARE
RESPONSIBLE FOR YOUR OWN ACTIONS.

Federal Trade Commission Required Disclaimer

To better define the term "average" and/or "typical"
results, we will attempt to collect results from
individuals that have completed courses, trainings,
programs, seminars, live presentations or any other
platform that can be construed as informational. It
is understandable that some individuals that have
purchased a course, product(s), service(s), tactic(s),
techniques and/or idea(s) discussed or described
may have never even used or opened the material,
therefore unfortunately would have no results at all.

All of the testimonials, stories, case studies and/or
presented results and any other supporting
materials related to the potential success by using
any of the course, product(s), service(s), tactic(s),
techniques and/or idea(s) discussed or described,
does not mean anyone current, past or in the future
will have any results at all. We do not guarantee
anything. There is no guarantee, either expressly,
implied, inadvertently offered or even suggested for
anyone purchasing and/or using our course(s),

product(s), service(s), tactic(s), techniques and/or idea(s) discussed or described.

The testimonials, stories, case studies and/or presented examples in any all of the Ligon Brothers materials represent what can be achieved, however it should be assumed by the student, client, reader, etc. that the results are based solely on the capability of the student and may not be reproducible by all.

The testimonials, stories, case studies and/or presented results and any other supporting materials related to the potential success are based on many variables and cannot be accurately quantified to meet the advertising standards set forth by the Federal Trade Commission (FTC) for determining the calculation of "average" and/or "typical results. Because of this it is unreasonable that any student should assume that any course, product(s), service(s), tactic(s), techniques and/or idea(s) discussed or described will produce any results at all especially if they choose not to use it properly and/or consistently.

Preface

This book was inspired by countless interactions that we've had over the last 15 years being involved in real estate investing.

Whenever I share my experience with someone, I'm always amazed by how intrigued they are with the thought of flipping houses. I'm talking about average, everyday people, not industry insiders, colleagues and associates.

These are people that I've met at social events, church, and networking events. It would almost seem as if people intuitively know that having proximity to real estate is having a proximity to money!

I can always relate to their want and desire to be involved in an industry that has had such a profound impact on my life and is such a large driver of the economy of the world. One thing that many of these people have in common is they always ask if there was a way they can flip one or two houses. I'm reminded of the intrigue that I had when I was first learning about real estate investing. I knew the potential that I saw in the life it could bring, so, it's no wonder to me that others would have the same vision about such a fascinating business.

After having all these interactions and conversations, I can say without a doubt that if each of these people had the confidence that real estate could replace and increase their current income, they would drop what they were doing and start immediately. But, what I have found is that people let fear, doubt, and insecurity stop them.

Most people, if asked, would agree that they have no doubt that real estate is a great wealth generator. Real estate has been a time tested and proven symbol of wealth since the beginning of time. However, doubt and fear comes into play when asked if they believe they can have part of this wealth generator. So, I realized, it's not doubt in the vehicle that they have; its doubt in the driver, in themselves.

What I know to be true is that success can be attained by anyone that has the desire, the motivation, and the dedication to follow a task to completion. I'm always telling new or prospective mentor students that come to us that if you're going to dedicate time and energy into building a business or venture, make sure it has the potential to fulfill the life you want to have.

This book will be simple, direct and to the point. Our hope with this book is to inspire and show anyone with the desire for more out of this life that is can be achieved through real estate investing. Real estate, without a doubt, has the potential to fulfill anyone's dream life and aspirations for success. Therefore, LYNK Wholesaling can be the great equalizer for those seeking advancement, success, and economic prosperity regardless of where they may be starting from.

Introduction

With our LYNK Real Estate System, the goal is to make real estate investing attainable to anyone and to simplify the process of graduating from newbie status to master real estate investor.

This system is a real life way for anyone from any background and any socioeconomic level to get started from zero and become super successful in real estate.

There were two questions that I always had when starting my pursuit of success through real estate:

1. "If it works so well, then why aren't more people successful?"

This question was the single biggest thing that stopped me from getting started sooner. All that I was able to come up with was that they must not have the drive. I did know that real estate has been the single greatest wealth generator and that it was a status of wealth since the beginning of time. I also knew that there are tons of successful investors, and if they could do it, then so could I!

2. "If the gurus' courses work, then why can't I delay payment until I'm successful using their knowledge?"

This other question stopped me for several years from even buying any educational material at all, real estate or otherwise. I ended up trying to connect the dots from multiple free sources. I'm sure you know what I'm talking about, using numerous websites and resources to learn everything you can without having to pay. At this point in my business, I wish I would have known back then that if you're good at something, you'll never do it for free.

The lesson here is that you will pay for knowledge in one of two ways: time or money. I now choose to pay for knowledge with money.

If you are anything like I was, you're probably looking at this situation all wrong. Think about this: we all want to make more money so that we can have more time to do the things we love, but we don't want to spend anything to learn how to make that money faster. Interesting, isn't it? It is time for to you change your thinking and begin to realize that paying for knowledge is, in effect, buying time in your life and shortening your time to become successful.

We want you to be able to live your best life, and we know that real estate is one of the best ways to make your dreams a reality.

If you are reading this book, I will assume that you are looking for a way to improve your future, a way you can make consistent income, but in an industry that has the promise of unlimited possibilities and excitement that a day job doesn't have. Maybe you are looking for a way to make a little extra income from home or on the side like we were when we started.

Maybe you want more; you want the bigger house, the nicest car, the dream vacation. That's great too, and is excellent motivation to keep your pursuit towards ultimate success alive. Maybe you've even tried and failed, or have even been scared to start in real estate. I've been there, and you shouldn't let that stop you from trying again.

The steps, ideas, and practices that we'll be telling you about are the exact things that we have used in our own business, starting from the first house we bought many years ago, and that have got us where we are now. I can tell you with 100% certainty that anybody with the drive and determination to succeed can do so using these formulas and teachings if they're willing to do the work.

It's been a hard-fought battle along the way through the market crash of the mid-2000s. Despite the setbacks, drive and determination kept us committed to pursuing what we knew could become the vessel to our dream lives.

Having been a part of over (at the time of the writing of this book) 500 flipped properties, we've had the privilege of flipping everything from vacant lots, burned out shells of houses, to million-dollar homes.

I only tell you of these successes to push the point that this lifestyle is attainable to anyone. You must take advantage of the current thriving market we are in before it changes. Get started now!

We come from very humble beginnings. My brother and I did not grow up in a life of privilege. At a young age, we had to drop out of school in order to work and help support our family as we grew up. Our success was only accomplished through hard-fought battles, including breaking through the beliefs that this kind of life and success wasn't attainable without the proper credentials.

You can rest assured that if we can do it, then so can you! We were able to start this business while working regular jobs and just trying to make ends meet. The one thing we did have was a deep desire to succeed and have more. We wanted enough income to help family and friends in our lives, and to be able to contribute to causes we care about. Sometimes the greatest part of success can be to ability to give and to help others.

If this story seems familiar, if it resonates with you, or if you can relate, then I want you to understand that you are able to be successful, too. Real estate investing is within your reach if you take the time to invest in yourself, invest in your knowledge, apply that knowledge and take action on a daily basis.

For a quick review on what we are doing:

There are two types of real estate investing that people think of when you get started:

- Fixing flips, doing rehabs—due to its popularity, that's probably the first thing you think of, though it's a little difficult to start it unless you have money. And if you don't have the experience, that can be problematic

- Wholesale–traditional wholesale has been seemingly the lowest barrier entry point to getting into real estate investing. You probably have seen a lot of stuff about wholesaling as an entry point for beginning in real estate investing. Not much money is needed in wholesaling as in fixing flips.

It has become more expensive getting leads and attracting motivated sellers. Regardless, in wholesale and fixing flips, we have been able to evolve past the standard ways of getting started in real estate. We are going to share with you the secrets that we have discovered as a result of being able to close over 500 deals down here in the brutal Miami market of South Florida.

If you have ventured out and failed at all in the past, in doing some type of real estate or in being an entrepreneur of any kind, it is not your fault. There are a lot of things holding people back, such as your working conditions, your community or previous negative experiences that make it difficult or frightening to continue in real estate.

If you've been concerned in the past or even now that you just can't succeed in real estate, I want you to put those fears to rest and have an open mind as to what possibilities are really out there.

We are going to go over and dive deep into all the things that we have learned over the course of our business. You definitely must understand that you can make a difference and that you can get involved in real estate, regardless of what your preconceived notions have been in the past of what is possible or not possible for you.

One thing we can all agree on is that you are not reading this book for me to prove to you that real estate can work. That is way beyond me or any of us. That's been proven, time and time again, as the number one wealth generator in the world.

What we want you to grasp from this book is you are able to do it. You are able to go out there and get started in real estate. Regardless of the things you perceive as road-blocks–whether they are money, credit, or resources–it is possible to begin in real estate and to attain success from it.

Chapter 1. It is Attainable

The first thing that I will discuss in this book is "Our Weird House Flipping Niche That Made Us $30k in 30 Days" and how to *ethically* use someone else's hard work and experience to do it. I will walk you through how we developed all the strategies we use to this day, explaining the whole process that we went through in discovering and putting this system together.

I am NOT saying to you that you are going to make $30k in your first month from simply reading this book. You cannot jump into this field and become a millionaire overnight; this isn't what this book is about.

This book is about showing that it is attainable to succeed in real estate if you are dedicated. Becoming an investor, defined as *"a person or organization that puts money into financial schemes, property, etc. with the expectation of achieving a profit,"* and a financially successful person are not taught in most families. In actuality, it's not taught in schools or colleges or universities. In fact, if you told most people that you were going to invest your earnings on a real estate investor course, they would probably tell you it was a scam.

This is the lie that society perpetrates on us all that if you dare to go against the norm and pursue something that can make you rich quickly or easily that it must be some kind of scheme. The truth is that society is set up to keep you and me in the middle class.

If you follow the path that society has laid out for the masses, then you will end up being a slave to the hump days and TGIF's of life, living really for only 2 days out of your week, the weekend. And if you're lucky enough to make it through working for the best 45 years of your life, you'll be granted the luxury of retiring with barely enough income to be on a tight budget and get your senior discount at your favorite local restaurant.

I knew that I didn't want to end up like this, and was willing to do or spend money on anything that would give me more time with my family and doing the things I love. So, I began educating myself and breaking away from the constructs of society.

Schools won't teach you how to make substantial money, how to invest, or how to become rich through different revenue streams. Society, in fact, frowns upon that pursuit in many instances. Just think all of the things that you've heard throughout your life referring to money. Most are probably in the negative. In most cases, when people speak about someone who is wealthy, it's from the position of disdain. Even the sayings "filthy rich" and "dirty money" illustrate the way that it has been ingrained in us to describe money and wealth with a negative attitude since day one.

It's time to break that mold. There is a prosperous life available and within reach for anyone to obtain, as long as they have the boldness to reach out and take the reins.

If you want to be successful, truly successful in real estate investing, you will have to subdue any of the negative beliefs about becoming wealthy and about money that you may have. It's okay to want the full and prosperous life of your dreams. You need to start looking at money as a conduit, as means to an end. It is something to be used and taken advantage of before it is lost. You should want to have money, but don't save money just to save it; you should save money in order to invest.

Becoming an investor starts by investing in yourself! Read that sentence again. It is vitally important to your ultimate success that you understand that being an investor starts with a mindset and ends with the constant pursuit of multiplying your dollars.

I argue that you become an entrepreneur the moment you spend your first dollar investing in your own mind and knowledge base. No one can go from zero to a million, or even hundred million, dollar business or portfolio without first investing in the knowledge to make that possible. In order to prove this point, let's look at some examples of the most lucrative of day jobs you could have, such as being an attorney, doctor, engineer, or computer scientist. What all of these individuals that have chosen to pursue these careers have in common is spending, in many cases, hundreds of thousands of dollars on their education.

Another area in general is advertising; this is the same principle at work. It involves a company investing in itself through promoting who they are, what they do, and how they can benefit others.

In the same way, if you want to make becoming a real estate investor a reality, you will have to invest in yourself, which requires both time and money. There is no way around this equation. Once you realize and accept this, you will begin to overcome the confines in your mind about money. You will begin to see money differently, and to use it as fast as possible to shortcut the learning curve to success.

This is the concept of buying and multiplying time. All of us have the same amount of time in a day, so how is it that some of us are able to achieve more? The answer is simple. We have figured out how to compress the time it takes for us to get to the next step in our lives. This shortens the success curve, and crowns us the successful, productive entrepreneurs in life.

The act of buying knowledge can exponentially shortcut and close the proximity between you and your ultimate success. It does this in many ways. One crucial way is by allowing you to avoid mistakes. Mistakes would cost you valuable time! The cost of a mistake is a lot more than the cost it would be to avoid it.

A mistake can not only cost you monetarily, but it can also cost you in time. This is the reason why buying knowledge is so important. If you could save 2, 3 or even 5 years of grinding and piecing together information from a hundred different sources, what would that be worth to your life?

I hope you truly understand the importance of this concept of buying time and avoiding mistakes. It can literally take years off of your pursuit toward success if done properly! Put this one thing into practice, and you will be well on your way to achieving your goals.

All of these factors are incredibly important to making your goal of being a real estate investor a reality. Before anything, you must first become an investor in your mind by understanding and having a different relationship with money. The easiest way to do this is by becoming an investor in yourself.

If you're not willing to spend money on your own education, you will never be willing to risk it on an actual investment.

Luckily, real estate can be very low risk and doesn't require you to possess a lot of capital to get started. However, if you do not have the mindset of an investor and haven't taken the time to invest in your own knowledge base, then you will not be prepared for what's to come.

Mindset is Key!

Chapter 2: The Investor Mindset

In order to be a successful real estate investor, you will need to transform your mindset. You have to drop the beliefs and negative perceptions that have kept you in the position that you're currently in. A lot of the traditions and traits that we are instilled with as we grow up are the very things that keep us from reaching our greatness.

For example, if you look at any one of the industry leaders in our country and the world, you will never hear him or her saying "don't take risks." Instead, they talk about how to mitigate risk. The underlying message here is that they know that there is no way to continue as a leading investor in any industry without risk. The game then becomes of one of how to reduce risk as much as possible.

I hate to say it, but the gurus out there lie. There are various courses on traditional wholesaling out there that say you can start doing deals with no money. However, in reality, it is very difficult to start doing deals in the real world. For instance, you need deposits. Although they may say simply to put in a small deposit of $10, that doesn't work when you're competing for deals and everyone else is putting up real deposits, especially when the seller has an attorney. So, it is imperative to insure you understand what work you're getting into.

As an entrepreneur, you must realize and understand that the mindset of instant gratification must come to an end. If you started out in the same position as I did, with an hourly job collecting a weekly paycheck and exchanging your time for money, then that is the only life you know. That is the life of instant gratification. You exchange an hour of your time for an hour of pay, a week of your time for week of pay, a month of your time for month of pay and this continues for the rest of your life unless you decide to you break that mold.

Entrepreneurship begins in your mind. It starts with a seed that oftentimes you were unaware was planted, until one day it just bursts, causing you to become unsatisfied with the status quo. If you've been blessed with this desire, you must nurture, feed and become obsessed with growing this seed to maturity.

Continue to nurture this seed with information. The mere fact that you're reading this book, that you are a seeker of knowledge, puts you ahead of millions of other people on this planet that are not even willing to take this one small step-this step towards change.

Don't let the lies of disbelief, of low self-esteem, and lack of confidence stop you from realizing that you can become an entrepreneur. You can become a real estate investor, regardless of where you may be starting your path.

You may be thinking, "Yeah, but I don't have any money," "I don't have any time," or "I don't have any credit." These are thoughts of scarcity. You need to be thinking from a perspective of abundance! Instead of thinking that you don't have those things, you need to be finding out ways to obtain them. This is a key factor in becoming an entrepreneur and changing your mindset.

Every time we sit down with students that have taken our LYNK Real Estate program, they are always surprised that they indeed can find the money or time to become a real estate investor. There are many factors that can impact or influence one's goal toward becoming an entrepreneur. For example, ask yourself this question: Do you own the latest and greatest phone, shoes, and car? If you do, then you're probably not practicing the investor mindset.

You must be honest with yourself: Why did you purchase that phone, car or pair of shoes? Did you buy them for yourself because you genuinely wanted them, or did you feel the need to have "the best" items out there? If you are buying these items in order to make yourself appear cooler, to impress your friends, or to follow the latest trends out there, then you need to realize that you're living a life for other people.

This may be a difficult conclusion to come to, but it is important for you to realize in order to make the changes necessary to change your mindset. To become a successful entrepreneur, you need to achieve a higher level of understanding than your peers. They will not be willing to step out and risk their time, energy, and money in order to achieve greatness in their life. The peers and mentors that you need to be pursuing in order to be successful will not be impressed by physical assets; they will be more interested in your abilities and skillset.

Therefore, stop investing in meaningless social activities and trends, and focus on what others are unwilling to do. Go without the latest and greatest phone, shoes, etc. because these gadgets and objects are not investments; they are liabilities in your life and liabilities to your future success. Sacrifice it now so you can have it all later.

Your resources, especially as you try to create success as a real estate investor, should be put to better use instead of paying for a brand! If you have a hundred extra dollars, you should really be buying $100 worth of education. If you have an extra $1,000 dollars, you should buy $1,000 of education, and so on and so on. Do this until you're in a position that you have enough knowledge to turn that knowledge into action and start making money with your newfound abilities.

Once your new abilities start making you some money, you should implement and practice the One Thing Rule. Simply stated, you should focus solely on the one new strategy you have learned to make money and focus only on that strategy until you have a stockpile of cash.

Once you have a successful source of cash flow, you start this process over again, only this time, you're one step higher up the ladder than before. Again, you need to be investing into your knowledge base. If you have an extra $2,000, then you should invest $2,000 into learning your next step. This idea is the opposite of the instant gratification mindset. Instead of having you exchanging your time for money, you're exchanging your dollars for time in the form of knowledge and shortcuts.

You should be doing this as often as humanly possible while building your "one thing." Set that machine in motion, building it to its full capacity. Then, start duplicating that process with the next step in your plan that can make you even more money.

As an example, in our LYNK Real Estate System, you would start with LYNK Wholesaling, move to LYNK Flipping, then LYNK Fix-N-Flip, and so on.

The most important part of this rule is to have a plan. I say often to make sure that whatever you're getting into, whatever course you're taking, whatever program you're thinking about following, that it has the capacity to fulfill the life that you want. Make sure there is a path in that program, in that course, or with that mentor, so that you can progress along as you grow in knowledge and experience.

I'm often asked: "Can't I just go on YouTube and do it on my own?" In short, yes. But why would you want to do that? It is possible to get a lot of great information free on many social media sites and you should be doing this, however, it is impossible to replace a structured course or, especially, a great mentor with this information. A mentor can serve as a way to stay accountable as well as be a reliable authority in times of uncertainty. You can't call YouTube when a deal is falling apart.

There will always be someone who has their business or craft further along than you do. So, you can and should always be seeking to learn from these people. Join mastermind groups and become accountable to someone who can give you an accurate direction and help you succeed.

The first step in developing your investor mindset was acknowledging the seed that was planted in your mind and that you are nurturing it right now by even choosing to read this material. However, it will be a daily struggle to maintain a positive mindset and to maintain the motivation that it will take to overcome the pull of society. That pull is trying to get you in-line with everyone else. You must resist this at all costs.

One of the great things about the era we live in is the availability of knowledge and vast amount of sources of motivation. This can be easily obtained online, especially through social media, and you should take full advantage of that on a daily basis by following like-minded individuals and staying motivated. However, it is vitally important for you to commit actual money in order to invest in your knowledge and the business you're trying to grow. Above all else, your money will keep you accountable. Don't be a cheapskate with your future. Pay the price now so you can pay any price later!

Let me illustrate what I mean by telling a quick story. I have a hundred very similar stories, so I'll leave names out, but they all go something like this: A new prospective student comes to talk to us. They tell us they've been learning about real estate online, all the social media platforms, on the video platforms that are available, basically all of the free advice that you can get all over the internet.

Then, they proceeded to tell us that they're just not sure if they can trust what they're being taught. They don't know if those people are actually doing any of the things that they're teaching, and feel like there are a lot of things being left out. We're then told that they started to do a few of the activities that they've learned about. Maybe this means they made a few phone calls on some properties, they've gone to see a few properties.

What happens next is they get to a point where they're not sure what the next step is. This makes them frustrated and discouraged. They feel this because they put so much time into learning but they're still not sure what to do next. Their motivation goes out the window and they start to fall back into the line that "it just can't be done," they don't have what it takes, and it's only for people with money or credit, etc...

We have identified two factors as the greatest contributors to this de-escalation of motivation. They are the following: getting started on the wrong thing and, most of all, lack of accountability.

These factors are extremely important to understand when it comes to changing your mindset. Accountability is vital to your ultimate success. If I had to pinpoint one thing that would have the biggest impact on someone just starting out, this would be that one thing– accountability! The difficult aspect of accountability is that people will seldom enforce it upon themselves.

Our minds are a powerful thing, and the excuses and justifications we can create for failures can be addictive. This is one reason why we talk so much about the need to pay for proximity, to pay for education and knowledge. It's our experience that there is one thing that has the best chance of a person keeping themselves accountable, and that is their money.

Start putting your money on the line, and you'll see how fast your commitment will follow.

I can tell you this from personal experience and from the experiences of many others. This obligation can be a powerful motivator that pushes people over the edge to commit to the endeavors they're pursuing.

Nobody wants to waste money, and wasted knowledge equals wasted money, especially if you paid for it. Trust me in this, and see if it doesn't open the floodgates of inspiration, determination and motivation in your pursuit of becoming a LYNK Real Estate Investor.

This journey starts with the investment in yourself and preparing your mind for the things to come. Money will return to you, so invest it in your future, not your present. Don't trust the masses when it comes to money and monetary advice or you'll end up just like them. It's time to expand your mindset, to expand your idea of what investing truly is.

Buy time whenever possible and you will be well on your way to a better life. A life of security and excitement, a life of love and importance, a life of being able to help others you love and care for. The life of freedom and abundance that we all want and deserve is attainable.

Pursue your dreams at all costs! Don't let past failures or disappointments determine your future; you just didn't have the right information...yet!

Too much wrong information...

Chapter 3: Success is a Choice

Could it really be that easy? Can I simply choose to be successful? Relatively speaking, yes you can. Let me explain how it really can be this simple.

Picture yourself coming to the end of your day. The day is winding down, you're getting ready for bed, but you remember you have an early appointment tomorrow. You need to get up a little earlier than normal, let's say 5:30 a.m., so you set your alarm for 5:30 a.m. You go on about your evening routine, eventually make it to bed and no sooner do you close your eyes it seems like your alarm is buzzing.

At this point, you have a choice. You can easily hit the snooze button, decide to cancel the whole appointment because it's too early, or get up on time to show up to that appointment on time. This is where success begins. With every small decision you make, you can choose to be successful.

This may seem like an understatement to your interpretation of success, however, if you can wrap your mind around this concept, then success becomes a game. Who doesn't like to win a game?

Let's dive deep and uncover all the ways we can build and choose success on a daily, weekly, and monthly basis. I often talk about setting up successes in your routine. An example of this would be as relating to real estate; if your goal or dream is to own 500 units as rental income and you are starting at zero, you would only consider yourself successful once you get 500.

In order to have more success in your life, you need to set up successes along the way. For instance, when developing your plan to get your first unit, you should have built-in successes to achieve on the path there. This might look like setting smaller goals for yourself, like a goal of contacting 100 property owners and trying to make a deal. Maybe it's a goal of making 10 offers on properties to see if that will result in one deal. Whether you're getting involved in LYNK Wholesaling or you want to be completing 10 closings a month once your business is established, you wouldn't consider yourself a failure if in 3 months you're not at that main goal yet. The objective here is to have micro goals, short-term goals, and long-term goals.

To ensure success, you must also have plans for achieving these goals. You should have micro plans to achieve your micro goals and so on and so on. This is what success looks like on a day-to-day basis.

It's easy to look at someone that has millions in the bank, a ton of properties and would by all rights be considered very successful and have a picture in your mind saying that is success. The picture you should be painting is the day-to-day successes that got that person there.

Once you start to understand this way of thinking, it will be much easier for you to grasp the concept of choosing success on a day-to-day basis. Every choice you make, even something small and seemingly insignificant, will either lead you closer to or farther from you're short and long-term success.

One of our students took this concept to a whole new level and ended up wildly successful. She decided to follow these instructions to the "T" and apply them to every aspect of her life. From making her bed in the morning to flossing her teeth at night, everything became an opportunity to be successful. In order to be more efficient and create more time to pursue real estate, her activities at work also became mindful choices to continue being successful.

Once you start implementing these ideas, it will begin to snowball into everyday successes. Ultimately, it will break the daily grind of monotony and change your perspective of your routine.

Being conscious of setting up a winning series of events is going to be extremely consequential for maintaining your motivation, drive and determination for completing the task at hand. In the beginning, I suggest a progressive approach similar to working out. You start light, you build, you challenge, and you overcome the next obstacle.

If this is a new concept for you, make sure to start with something easily attainable but continually challenging. Every step after the first should become progressively harder to accomplish. If you're setting a goal on your first go-round of doing 10 of something, the next time needs to be 12 or 15.

Something else that is vitally important during this process is that you must be hard on yourself. You must expect more from yourself than you would expect from others and have no choice but to deliver. You have to hold yourself to a higher standard than anyone else would expect of you and that you would expect of anyone else.

If you're serious about making a difference in your life and moving ahead in your new business or venture that you're pursuing, then you have to get seriously hard on yourself, honest with yourself and be willing to hold yourself accountable. You can't function at the same level of accountability and motivation as the rest of society if you want to rise above them. If you want an extraordinary life, you have to do extraordinary activities.

I also want you to look at success being a choice from a little bit of a different angle. Understanding the simple fact that you are pursuing a life worth the pursuit is in itself a success. You choosing and desiring to be successful in real estate investing, which can deliver the resources needed to live your dream life, is in and of itself a choice to be successful.

I want you to understand that the only way to fail from this point on, in this new adventure in your life, is to give up. That alone should motivate you. Understanding that as long as you continue the activities, regardless of how long they take to reach your considered level of success, you cannot fail.

Embrace the fact that you are making choices that society at large will not make. You pursuing, dedicating and changing your mindset is a success on its own. You are separating yourself from the rest of the pack by investing in your knowledge base and skill set that you will use to build your empire.

Never measure your achievements against those of others; instead you should use the achievements of others as benchmarks of what can be accomplished in your own life. Most people know, without a doubt, that real estate is a tried and true method and that wholesaling and flipping houses can make massive amounts of money. This realization should give you the confidence to be committed unequivocally to your success in this endeavor.

Seeing the achievements of others that are more successful, regardless if they are colleagues, competitors, mentors, or peers, should give you the utmost confidence that you too can achieve that same or even greater level of success in your own life. Fear of the unknown is what stops so many from achieving what is, in all respects, the success that is within arm's reach.

Fear or lack of confidence will stop success dead in its tracks every time. It will stop you from buying that bigger deal, from buying your first rehab, or from putting a deposit on your first wholesale deal. It will even stop you from buying a course or mentorship to learn how to do the things your heart desires.

This is why success is a choice. It is a choice in everything you do, from waking up on time the showing up to work on time and I don't just mean "showing up." I mean being present, being engaged and going into every day with a mindset of total domination. If you're not the best employee that your boss has, you will never be the best employee for yourself.

Learn the traits and develop the character that you will need to be successful on your own, and do it while you're getting paid at your job. Don't wait to go out on your own and realize you lack the proper motivation, desire, determination, and obsession for success that you will need in order to achieve higher levels of wealth.

As I mentioned, start looking at this as a game, a very serious game and your goal should be to win at all costs. There's only one player in this game. Your only competition is yourself, and your goal is to win and win big. If you can overcome the obstacles, beliefs, and misbeliefs that have been drilled into your mind your whole life, then you can achieve anything you want.

When you first start out on your journey in real estate investing, it is going to be primarily about knowledge, acquiring knowledge any way you can. The way to win at this stage of the game is to understand that knowledge equals time. If the knowledge that you're investing time and money into learning can get you deals quicker and help you avoid mistakes more often, this means you are effectively buying extra time in your life by closing your proximity to success.

Let's face it, we all want success and to be successful as fast as possible. We want to pay our bills with ease and to have money left over to enjoy life to the fullest.

I'm sure you would agree that if you were going to do something on your own that would take you a hundred tries but I told you a way of doing it that would only take you 25 tries, you would hold that information as something extremely valuable for many reasons.

It would be extremely valuable because it would save you time and all of the extra tries of attempting to do that thing, as well as the costs involved in attempting to do it all those additional times. Knowing this, you will be more productive at closing your proximity to success and effectively buy time in your life.

It's time to make an action plan for your choices in life. Be purposeful in all the things you do, and this desire will meet you right where you are at today. You don't need to prepare anything first. You don't have to get your whole life in order first; you can use these principles to do those very things. Then, you can use them to build your real estate investing business.

Chapter 4: Our Success Story

The LYNK System will work for everyone, including:

- Seasoned investors looking to add more revenue and take advantage of every lead
- Novice investors that are just starting out and have only done a few deals
- Newbie investors and wholesalers that have never done a deal.

We created this system so that anyone and everyone could become real estate investors. We were just two regular guys that were looking for extra ways to make money when we got involved in real estate. We have always wanted to work for ourselves and always had that desire to create something to be able to move into the next bigger picture for our lives and a better scenario than just a 9-5 job.

Let me tell you about the path that led us to the amazing discovery that would ultimately lead us to success.

Something that has always driven me to become successful is one of my earliest and most vivid childhood memories. I had to be around five or six years old. Our family had just woken up from being all crammed from sleeping in the back of our suburban truck. We were packed up and ready to move into our new house, but that place was a hazard and we couldn't sleep in there. It was in an unkempt neighborhood surrounded in high grass.

I just remember getting up out of the truck and entering the house to see that it was bare, no furniture or anything. I remember seeing my mom, sitting on an old stool in front of a dirty window and leaning on the windowsill and just eating a bowl of cereal. Those images were etched in my mind.

As I got older, this memory stuck with me and I made up my mind that I did not want my kids to have that kind of memory growing up. That memory has been my driving force.

One day back in the early 2000s, I remember I was driving down the street when I heard an ad on the radio. It piqued my interest. I heard a man saying that you can buy a house with zero money and no closing cost. He talked about "no money down," fix and flip investing. I said to myself, "I hope that works because I don't have money to put into it anyway."

I had already been kicking around the idea of real estate at the time, buying random real estate courses on ways to invest in real estate, so I called the man from the ad and ordered the course with my last couple thousand bucks. I wanted to learn how to get involved in real estate because I didn't know much about that industry. This course actually properly got me started on the basics of real estate.

We then started looking for houses, but we still worked at our full-time job, just squeezing out as much cash as we could. I started looking for houses on my time off and on the weekend. It took several months, but finally I found our first house. I was able to get into it with no money and without paying closing cost. The house needed some work, so it was a good learning experience for how the process worked.

We both saw our closing succeed, and became more involved in this business. We were able to see what goes into this process, so we tried to rehab the house ourselves. It took a lot of money and a lot of time. We were also facing many issues, such as putting repairs and materials on credit, managing workers that don't show up, and paying mortgage payments and insurance payments. It was a disaster, as you can see. However, it was a process we learned from and it was working for us for a time.

We got a few more of these houses and were able to make some extra money. Even though it was time-consuming, things began to look up for a bit. Then, the unthinkable happened.

During the mid-2000s, the recession hit and the economy crashed (the worst recession in 100 years). We were in the middle of rehabbing five houses when the real estate bubble burst. Due to the foreclosure crisis, our house values dropped by 50% and we lost the houses, putting us over $2,000,000 in debt. It seemed like the world was on pause for the next couple years.

You know when you talk about sleepless nights, wondering where your next paycheck will come from, cringing when the phone rings, completely stressed out? This was back when I owned a fax machine and my fax machine didn't have a ringer that I could turn off. Every time it rang, I would get so badly startled that I literally put duct tape over the ringer speaker. It was crazy. It was a really scary scenario being that stressed and worried all the time in the middle of the worst recession in a hundred years.

We were struggling to get by like millions of other people, and we were under the impression that everybody was going through the same kind of problems we were. It wasn't until a friend from our real estate dealings mentioned to us that he knew somebody locally down here that was doing well in real estate and was still making money even in this crazy down market.

So, he introduced us to the local mentor that was wholesaling houses. This encounter was our first entry into the wholesale world. After we met this guy, we started going to some meetings and discovered what wholesaling is all about. We understood a bit about fixing flips, but we didn't know about wholesaling. Simply, a wholesale deal is where you would go get a property under contract and sign a contract with the seller. Then, during the inspection period, you have some time where you are able to flip that property to another buyer, flip that contract to another investor, and they close on it. In the end, you make money in the middle of it. This is really condensed version of goes on in wholesaling.

We began learning about how that process worked and started to understand that it is possible to make money in a down market within real estate and if you're not taking market risk. With this information, we started doing wholesaling.

We learned many wholesaling tactics from that mentor. He showed us a new way of doing things. We then started doing very well in real estate. Mind you, we were still working jobs and piecing things together. The economy was also still pretty tough, but we jumped into this field with both feet. Hammering out some deals, meeting at 5:00 a.m. in the morning to formulate offers and review properties, making phone calls on our lunch hour, getting together after work at one of our houses, putting offers in and following up on phone calls, figuring out our marketing plans, I mean everything that goes into developing a wholesale business, we did it.

We were doing so well that we were invited to conferences to speak and be shown as success stories for this mentor. A lot of business developed out of how well we were doing and it was great. We were closing on lots of deals, and it really took us out of the rat race, so to speak.

Overtime, however, we started to see that there were some holes in this system. We definitely identified some major problems we were running into. Some of the core things we saw were serious chinks in the armor of wholesaling, even at a decent entry point into the world of real estate.

One of the chinks in the wholesaling armor we ran into was deposits—nobody talks about deposits. At some point, you have to put up deposit on a deal. You can't hold that off. If you're trying to close a deal and you get a buyer, somebody must have a deposit in order to close a deal. Because we didn't know this, our deals didn't close on time. Different issues can happen, like the sellers not being ready to move, or title issues where the property is not ready to be sold in time because there is some kind of court order needed.

We had four to five deals that were not closing on time and we had deposits on all of these deals. Our money was just sitting in escrow, thousands of dollars sitting on escrow that we couldn't use. Because of this, we started having cash flow issues. We're advertising and having to keep all this money sitting escrow account and deals are not closing on time. On top of that, we still had to advertise on more deals and that gets really expensive when you're sending thousands of letters, postcards and internet advertising.

There is a serious outlay of cash needed in order to keep deals going and keep the wholesale engine moving. This is even more of a problem when you run into other problems, such as closing delays, and that money is just sitting around because you don't have access to it. This was a massive problem that we were always trying to figure out a way to get past.

Another chink in the armor we recognized was advertising. When we spent money in doing advertising and we took our buyers to a property, sometimes nobody would want the deal, for whatever reason. However, if we could not sell a deal, we had to give it back, which would add to the cost of losing deals and not being able to sell them, raising our advertising acquisitions cost per deal.

However, something happened to us, almost by coincidence, and we capitalized on it. We had this deal in the Fort Lauderdale area, and we took a couple of buyers to see the property. One buyer, in particular, said he wanted something in a different area from where we had our house located. This prompted me to call a colleague that I remembered had a deal around that part of town. We partnered with that colleague and helped him sell his deal to our buyer, and boom—the first LYNK wholesale deal was completed. That was when LYNK was created.

From there, we continued to resell deals and added it into our practice. It blew our minds that we could actually do that, fill in the gaps of our wholesale business by selling other wholesalers' deals. I wish we had known this when we started. This information would have helped us avoid so much aggravation and many lost deals.

Wholesaler   You   Cash Buyer

Needless to say, we started reselling deals as much as we possibly could after discovering this method. We are the billing wholesaler in the middle; we are the one connecting the dots. Our buyer (the black hat dude) is looking for the deal. It's a win-win for everybody!

The buyer gets a deal he wants because we have access to more deals than they do. The wholesaler sells a deal that he couldn't sell on his own. He makes money, we make money, and the buyer gets his deal, then fixes it and sells it to make money. It's a win-win-win for everyone!

Naturally, we became obsessed in selling other wholesalers' deals to fill in cash flow, and it turned out to be massive amounts of cash flow. We were able to duplicate this system over and over again.

After the success of LYNK Wholesaling, the next thing we did was we started framing our checks. We picture framed our first 30 deals and put it on a wall.

These were our first 90 days deals, about $140,000 in deals. Since then, it's turned into a massive business edition for us and an amazing thing that we stumbled on to.

We did a bunch of stuff the right way, but we also made a lot of mistakes. Though I believe that mistakes are part of business, especially when you are learning from scratch, we want you–the reader of this book–to understand that it is totally possible to make money doing this with no money out of your pocket and no credit.

This system works for anybody at any experience level in real estate. It makes it possible to wholesale without investing huge amounts of time because of the niche that it is. There is nothing else like it, and it's a new way to wholesale houses. All you need is to have the desire to succeed.

We did a lot of things the hard way for way too long, including:

- Starting off advertising for deals
- Chasing down sellers
- Competing for the same leads as all the other wholesalers
- Losing deals because of inexperience due to not enough buyers
- Leaving money on the table–basically, when you don't know what you don't know, you don't make the money that you could have made; if we knew about LYNK Wholesaling earlier, we would have made a lot more money earlier

- Spending a lot of time and energy, learning real estate, and doing things almost backwards.

So, after years and years, we figured out things the hard way, but you do not have to do things the hard way. You can just "cheat" and get started the easy way. The easy way is by copying what works.

"Model What Works"

Chapter 5: The Three Secrets

This section encompasses the core of this book. I will go over three secrets that we have uncovered through our journey. You can use this information and implement it on your path.

SECRET #1: How to ETHICALLY Steal the Hard Work and Advertising Dollars of Other Wholesalers and Get Paid in the Process

I emphasize "ethically" because everything we do is ethical.

SECRET #2: How to Use Our PROVEN LYNK Wholesaling System to Flip Your First Deal in Less Than 30 Days

This is important. You want to know that you can keep this thing rolling. Nobody wants to waste time making and closing deals.

SECRET #3: How to Quickly Build a Massive Buyers List and Sell Them Other Wholesalers' Deals

This is the one that gets a lot of attention. This secret received so much feedback, and seeing people's reactions has been priceless.

Chapter 6: Secret #1

SECRET #1: How to Ethically Steal the Hard Work and Advertising Dollars of Other Wholesalers and Get Paid in the Process

Something I learned from Tony Robbins is, "If you want to achieve success, all you need to do is find a way to model those who have already succeeded."

It is very simple, just copy what's working. You do not want to be out there in the real estate world being the trailblazer. If you are a trailblazer and you are in front of the pack, trying new stuff and trying to find a new trail, you will end up in a ditch. We already ended up in that ditch and found the way out, and that is what we are showing you. You don't have to reinvent the wheel; just rely on what's proven to work. Use the wheel, don't reinvent it. Since real estate has been around for a long time, you don't have to. All you need to do is copy what's working.

Competitors

When I start a business, I like to see what kind of competition I have, if any. In real estate, there are two types of competitors:

1. Wholesalers (those who get the deals)
2. Buyers.

After seeing it over the years of doing this, however, we have identified through a vast amount of experience and through all the conversations we have had, wholesalers spend 60-70% of their time finding deals. They use the vast majority of their time going after deals while cash buyers spend 60-70% of their time managing rehabs, workers, materials, etc.

There is a large void between the two—the wholesalers going after deals and the buyers managing their work. Where we fit in this huge void is being the entity that is able to bring these two together. We are in between the wholesaler and the buyer, connecting them together. Don't get creative here and try to do something new; just fit into the hole.

As entrepreneurs, we have a tendency to start something new. However, in this scenario, don't get creative until you start making money. Plug into the traditional system that is already working. Once you have implemented that system and you are making money, then you can become creative.

Fill the Void

Student Testimony:

Hey guys, I want to give you an update on how things are going with me. I finished all of the training a couple of weeks ago, and started using everything I learned. I'm already getting a lot of great deals sent to me and actually working on my first offer. I'm super excited to keep going and getting this first deal completed. I can't believe how simple it was to get the access to all these deals and inventory. Thanks for everything, really guys. I'll keep you updated.

This system is truly working everywhere we have tried it. It has worked in every market that we've gotten students in, all around Florida, as well as in all of our first tests markets. We've been mentoring down here in person in our local market for a long time. After hearing the stories of people after using this system, we started rolling this out everywhere because we saw the way it made a difference in people's lives. It is improving people's lives, helping them to get out of debt and create a full-time real estate business for themselves.

Who Will This Work For?

You might be thinking to yourself: "I don't have the time," "I don't have this or that," or "I'm not that..."

But who will this system actually work for?

- It works for you if you are an entrepreneur. You have the entrepreneurial seed that needs to be watered and nurtured. It is not a mistake that you have picked up this book. It's not a coincidence you're learning something that you can get started with right where you are today.

- It works for full-time employees. Most, if not all, of our students have jobs. There's no way around it in this life. We all need money.
- It works for stay-at-home parents.
- It works for you if you have no prior experience in real estate (wholesaling, flipping, or rehabbing).
- It works for you if you don't have money.
- It works for you even if you have experience. If you are already in real estate or are a successful wholesaler, you can copy what we did and implement it sooner than we did to avoid a lot of mistakes.

The bottom line is that it doesn't matter what kind of stage you're in—it will work for you.

Where Do I Find Good Deals?

It is possible to find good deals and do so without money. The secret is to use other wholesalers' inventory, hard work, and advertising dollars. Do the following:

- Go to all the real estate associations (REI) in your general area and meet wholesalers.
- Utilize social media. Social media is also a great tool to expand networks. If you use it professionally, then social media can help you decrease the amount of time it takes you to be successful.
- Utilize real estate websites. There are thousands of websites on real estate. If you place a search on Google, it will bring up all of these websites. Search for the ones in your area. Since most of the people that have these websites are wholesalers, it is easy to get their contact information. Contact them, tell them

what you're doing, and befriend them when necessary. It's all about networking.

Start implementing these actions in all of these different areas, and you will see how the deals will start coming in. As stated in her testimony, our student started this with a full-time job, doing a little bit here and there, and then she started receiving deals.

The Blue Print

You find the wholesalers who have the house, partner with them. The buyers want the properties, connect the buyers with the wholesalers, they buy, you are paid for filling in the hole and everybody wins. It is very simple.

Chapter 7: Secret #2

SECRET #2: How to Use Our Proven LYNK Wholesaling System to Flip Your First Deal in Less Than 30 Days

The first thing we need to cover is the differences between the old way of wholesaling and our new way of wholesaling to better understand how this system works. To do this in your first 30 days, it is important for you to understand the way it used to be.

The old way of doing wholesaling included the following:

- Spending money on advertising. We would send out postcards, yellow letters, etc. We kept experimenting and advertising at the same time and both processes need money. You cannot effectively start and have recurring income in wholesaling without spending some money. Also, contrary to what anybody might tell you, there are issues with deposits. You must advertise and get steady on the deals. You've got to make tons of offers which take a long time to complete.

- Chasing down sellers.
- Taking 2-4 months to close a deal.
- Losing money due to inexperience.

None of these things is going to make you happy. You don't want to lose money, chase people around or any of the above.

There is a fresh, new, and better way that nobody else is doing things, and that is LYNK Wholesaling System.

The new LYNK Wholesaling way includes:

- No money on advertising.
- No chasing down sellers. You don't have to chase anybody down. The deals are freely, easily and willingly being sent as

soon as they are available. The hard work is done.

- No 2-4 month wait to close a deal.
- No money to lose. If you are not putting up in advertising or deposits, you have nothing to lose.

All the above will make you very happy.

Essential Tools for Getting Started in Real Estate

There are two essential things that you need to get started right now in real estate.

1. Determination and the Right Attitude

You must be determined. Nothing worth doing is going to come and be dropped in your lap. If you are looking for some get-rich-quick thing, we cannot help you. You need determination and the confidence that it can be done with minimal, if any, risk at all. The only risk now is the little bit of time that you would be putting in. Because you are starting a business that has this kind of potential to make money, it is a very easy risk to take.

You also need to have the right attitude. Every type of business needs the right attitude. You have to adopt the mindset of abundance and know that you are willing to do this.

2. LYNK Wholesaling System

This seems a little self-serving, but we want you to understand that we have been using this system for a long time now and, not only has it been working, but it will also continue to work.

Excuses

You may still be thinking that all these things sound amazing, but you don't have any experience in this field. The great thing about this system is that you don't need any experience. You don't have to know how to deal with sellers, you don't have to know how to sign a contract with a seller, and you don't have to understand the whole process before doing this. This is because you're not having to do it all by yourself. You are going to learn as you go along at the same time that you're making money. You can learn it without ever having to make a mistake because you are not the one putting all the pieces together or you're connecting the dots. Being experienced should no longer be an excuse to you. Get it out of your mind and move forward.

Some common excuses include the following:

Excuse: *I'm not a sales person...*

The wholesalers are out there doing the hard work and they will be sending you their deals. They are willingly sending you the deals. You don't have to coax or beg them for these deals because they are spending so much time getting them that, if they don't sell, it will damage their business.

Excuse: *I'm not an Internet marketer...*

It is actually quite easy. There is no complicated coding or computer programs that you need. It's all simple, basic tools that you already know how to use, such as Google to search for wholesalers and Google Docs to record your information.

Excuse: *I'm not an outgoing person, I don't like talking to people...*

You are not expected to be that type of person, to go out there and be speaking at length in front of people. You don't have to do that. All you have to do is simply have a conversation with some other people that are in real estate just like they were your friends. It's really easy. We have it all wrapped down to a science for you. You don't have to know anything special for you to do this.

Excuse: *I don't have any formal education...*

You don't have to have any formal education. All you need is to copy what works. Learn the process. As you are doing it, you are also learning.

Excuse: *I don't have any money...*

You don't need to have any money. You don't have to be chasing down deals. You don't need to be advertising and competing or any of this stuff.

This leads me to one of our students, Sam. He was not an outgoing guy, didn't have any formal education and didn't have a ton of money. He was just a normal, everyday guy. Then, however, he listened to our video.

Sam's Testimony

I was just working at a plumbing supply store house, supplying plumbers with their equipment. I listened to the video, put in practice what I have learned and in not more than six weeks, I got my first deal. Once you get started, it is really simple, everything is well explained.

This testimony drives the point home that you don't need to have tons of money or experience in order to start in wholesaling.

Chapter 8: Secret #3

SECRET #3: How to Quickly Build a Massive Buyers List and Sell Them Other Wholesalers' Deals

I love discussing this secret because I get so excited about the potential here for people to succeed. The question to ask is, "Where are the buyers?" This is because having massive buyers list will crown you king of the real estate mountain. Here are few ways of how to find the buyers:

1. County Property Appraiser Sites

This is one of the easiest ways to build a massive buyers list. Go to your county property appraiser website. Most of them now are on the internet, so use search for recent sales in the neighborhood that you want to find a buyer. Usually, they have a map that will come up when you click on the different parcels of land and houses. It will show you who owns the properties and when the last sale was made.

From there, you are going to look for properties that are owned by corporations of some kind. These are your cash buyers or buyers that are buying with hard money.

The great thing about these sites is that they are going to have their mailing addresses on the website. There are two things you can do: you can go drop your business card in those houses or you mail a letter, introducing yourself to them.

2. Local REIA Meetings

Experienced wholesalers that you're going to be dealing with will sometimes turn into buyers. As they get money, do new things and add into their growing business, their roles change in that business. Therefore, the more people you can meet in these meetings and add them to your list, the more your list will grow. Go to these meetings and hand them your cards. It is as simple as that.

3. Social Media

Social media is huge nowadays. It has become an easy way to grow your network. Go on social media and join groups, such as Facebook groups, specific to cash buyers.

A lot of wholesalers are in these groups trying to sell their deals, but then again, it's about being purposeful and intentional when you start to enter and interact in these groups. Eventually, you'll start to build your list.

These are the top three easiest, most attainable methods for anybody to build a massive buyers list. You can simply do these three from your computer!

You have what these buyers want and they're happy to oblige, so just take all the guesswork out. Again, you don't need to reinvent the wheel. All you have to do is model the LYNK system, a model what works.

So far, you have learned two essential things:

1. You know where the buyers are, and
2. You have what they want.

This is the motto we learned from Tony Robbins:

"Find a system that's being successfully done and copy it. That's the quickest way to success."

Chapter 9: LYNK Wholesaling

The true beauty of our LYNK Wholesaling system is that it is a progressive force of nature. We take you from zero to successes that are as big as your desire to achieve them.

We discovered and developed, through all of the transactions, all of the hard fought battles, all of the deals closed, and all of the trial and error of building our business, that it is a natural progression, a perfect storm of sorts.

What we've realized and what led us to eventually developing the LYNK Real Estate Investing System was that there is a precise path, a progressive path that can be followed to minimize the learning curve and risk of failure, thereby, maximizing the chances of success.

In other words, this system could be used to maximize profit and expand time by closing the proximity to being successful. If you knew without a doubt that you could accomplish more goals in less time and all you had to do was follow a step-by-step system, what would be stopping you?

Through painstaking experimentation, trial-and-error, and experience, we have identified the key factors and traits that, if combined in the right sequence and applied with the correct knowledge, can maximize the success rate of newbie real estate investors and wholesalers. Regardless of their starting point, our system is designed to allow everyone the same access to becoming a successful real estate investor.

When we first started flipping houses, we were only able to complete a few per year. It was very cash demanding, and it took time to manage the fix-n-flip process. We realized this was not the easiest thing to do while still working a 9-5 job. So, we then tried to wholesale a few houses while we were finishing some of the rehabs we were in the middle of.

With wholesaling, it seemed like we were spending even more money advertising, trying to find good deals and compete on offers than we were spending rehabbing houses.

When the unthinkable happened and the 2000's recession hit, we were struggling to stay afloat. This setback didn't stop us, however. We were determined to find a way back into real estate. Our options were slim since banks were not loaning, so we couldn't do any rehabs. We also didn't have the credit or cash for it anyway.

Our back was against the wall, so we sat down and decided we would dissect every aspect of real estate that we had learned and assess all the courses we'd bought. We knew there had to be a way, some way that we could get back into it without needing that time and money...

We did it! We came up with a way to make money—which was our main goal—flipping deals that we didn't have to get ourselves, deals that we never have to advertise to obtain. We created a way without having to talk with crazy sellers or chase them down, and without having to put deposits or risk our money. It was a simple idea, an easy idea. If only we'd thought about it a few years prior!

We realized that, as a wholesaler, you spend 60-70% of your time finding and cultivating deals, and as a buyer/rehabber, you spend 60-70% of your time managing and dealing with the projects.

Therefore, the only logical way to get started in real estate investing, without risk, money, advertising, chasing sellers, or spending tons of time is simply to start helping wholesalers and buyers/rehabbers get what they wanted. You need to be the Amazon or the Uber of real estate, aka the middleman.

Let's look at Amazon. When it first started, did Amazon go out and try to create millions of products to offer on its website? No! It just found people and companies who already had products and paired those products with buyers that wanted them!

The same is true with Uber (and many other huge companies). Did Uber go and buy a million cars to put on the road? No! They simply connected the people that had the product, being cars and trucks, to the people that need to use them. This is the best position to be in—all reward, no risk! Can't ask for more than that, right?

By starting out in a position like these businesses, we are putting ourselves in a position to maximize long term success. With this system, it sets us up for the least possible chance of failure so that we could make this a very lucrative career for ourselves.

By putting ourselves in the position of middleman, we can eliminate risk. By eliminating risk, we can eliminate caution. Eliminating caution means ridding ourselves of the natural fear factor that comes with any new endeavor.

For instance, if you were to start out in the standard wholesaling that maybe you hear about online, then, at some point, you would be required to put a deposit on the property you are trying to wholesale. Depending on what market you're in, that deposit can be anywhere from $100 to $10,000 or more, and you would need to have that money available in order to lock up a typical wholesale deal and be able to close that transaction.

Even though wholesaling is typically one of the lower risk ways of real estate investing, if you don't know what you're doing and you have a deposit on a property, there is always a risk of losing that deposit. If you don't have the proper language in your contract or addendum that your buyer signs to purchase that deal, for example, you could be stuck in the position where your buyer is able to get their deposit back, but you are not.

Regardless of these problems, we found a way to eliminate these fears. Without this fear of loss, we were able to put pedal to the metal and knew we had literally nothing to lose! It also allowed us to remove all of the risks that are inherent in traditional wholesaling.

Another problem we were able to solve by doing real estate this way was the issue of dividing our attention. Remember the One Thing Rule I previously mentioned? By focusing 90% of our time on one thing, we can achieve results way faster.

In our wholesaling system, we show you how to start in real estate investing without the need to risk losing a deposit or to risk money spent on advertising dollars. These are important aspects of our system because you do not want to be in a vulnerable position when you're still learning the basics about real estate. By any newbie, a loss of capital would be considered as a serious failure.

Even though it is somewhat inevitable to lose capital as you grow and have a large business, it becomes a business decision of whether or not you want to risk capital in order to close a little bit of a risky deal that might have a high payout.

When you're first starting out, however, this can be complete disaster. In the beginning, losing money can kill your ambition and motivation, and your will to persevere can all be extinguished with a single loss.

There is a better way–a way that you can gain the knowledge and experience needed to avoid costly mistakes when you're first starting out. You can do this while at the same time earning profit from real estate deals, and this is how the LYNK Real Estate progression starts.

Enter LYNK Wholesaling. This system is the starting ground for anyone looking to learn about real estate, earn some money while doing so, and have literally no risk, if done properly, in any transaction you're a part of. LYNK

Wholesaling is a way of building your network, your knowledge base, your experience, and your confidence, all while being able to profit from real estate transactions that you have no money tied up in.

Simply put, LYNK Wholesaling is the art of selling other wholesalers deals. I say it's an art because, as we developed this system and after having been a part of hundreds and hundreds of transactions, we have realized that there are a set of specific rules and tactics that will lead to almost guaranteed success if followed correctly.

When you're dealing with many different wholesalers and many different buyers, you need to understand certain principles that will allow you to maximize your position, protect your position in the transaction, and maximize profit in the deal for yourself. That's what this is all about after all, right? Profit!

We could literally write a whole series of books on all the different ways that we have found to accomplish this. Of course, all these ways are done legally and ethically because, above all, what you're building is your reputation as a reputable real estate investor and business professional. Never let a deal or profit compromise your network, your integrity, your reputation, or your ethics.

As previously mentioned, as you start out in wholesaling of any sort, your most powerful asset will be your buyers list. A large portion of your time when you're first starting should go toward building this list at all costs. You should never stop building this list. Again, this is the concept of the "one thing"–90% of your time goes to building you buyers list and 10% goes to finding already available deals in your market to piggyback.

The great thing about LYNK Wholesaling is that you can use this system anywhere. Even if you're in a rural area, you can apply these principles to your closest urban area and be able to profit off of deals that are nowhere near you!

One of the things that makes this wholesaling system a great entry point for beginners is the minimal requirements needed to start. You don't need a huge marketing budget to get deals or need to try to find motivated sellers. You don't have to worry about competing with offers on off-market properties.

All you really need to follow and succeed in this system is a positive attitude, motivation, and an unfailing will to succeed no matter what.

Your first step is simple; you need to start networking. If you think that you don't have enough experience or if you're a little bit introverted and don't know how to go out and talk with other professionals in real estate, let me tell you this: those things are not as important as you think.

Keep this in mind: as you're dealing with people in real estate, you will find that most, maybe not all but most of the people you'll be networking with, will be eager to help and forgiving to your lack of knowledge.

They will be much less hard on you than you would be on yourself. Don't worry if you say something that isn't exactly right or that may be incorrect. More often than not, they will just politely correct you, and this is what you want to have happen. You'll be learning from every encounter that you have on this path, so you should make it a point to have as many encounters as possible.

A lot of the valuable information that you can obtain from discussing real estate with people in your local area will be details and facts about your specific market. These details and facts will be things that you can't learn in any book or course because they are specific to your area. For example, that information could be warnings about neighborhoods to stay away from. It could be also be about major projects that will be happening that could affect property values in your location. Local professionals could even mention large buyers or organizations that you may want to be a part of and get to know.

In the event that maybe they don't mention these things, if you have confidence that the person you're speaking with is someone that is experienced and has been doing a lot of deals in your area, take the opportunity to ask them questions. Ask them what areas in your town they think are better than others and why. Ask them what price points do they see are moving and selling the best. All this information is going to help you to develop your knowledge of the market, which will in turn contribute to you being able to sound professional and knowledgeable as you're discussing your new business and the opportunities developing with prospective buyers and colleagues.

As you're out there talking with every person that you can find at your local meetings, local real estate investor associations, and business-to-business meetings, make sure to find out what they do specifically in real estate so that you can categorize them for the list that you will be building soon.

Most of them will fall into one of the following three categories: a wholesaler, a cash buyer, or a realtor. However, some could even be all three!

This distinction is important for several reasons. Each one of these different types of professionals will play a specific role in your LYNK Wholesaling business. Wholesalers will be the source where you get your inventory. This is one of the secrets in our LYNK Wholesaling System.

What makes having wholesalers contribute to your inventory so great is that you can literally piggyback off of the hard work, experience, risk, and marketing dollars of other wholesalers and use these things to build your own business without having to expend the same resources.

This is why we are so passionate about real estate. What other business on the planet has this much potential, where you can literally make millions of dollars, get into it without a formal degree, without even a high school diploma, not even need to advertise, or have to spend thousands of dollars developing programs? I can't think of any with the promise and potential of LYNK Real Estate Investing.

Right now, your goal is to meet as many wholesalers as you possibly can. They can be found at every local meeting near you, but you can also find them by going online to different social networks to find wholesaler groups.

As soon as you're able to, if your local real estate investing association has the ability to apply for a membership and maybe even set up a table at their meetings where you can be a vendor, I recommend you do so. As you meet wholesalers, you will be telling them that you have a strong buyers list and that you would like to remarket their deals to your buyers and do some type of partnership with them. Ask them for permission to market their deals and find out if there any specific things you need to know regarding how they do business so that you have an understanding and knowledge on how to handle their deals with your buyers.

Through our extensive experience in real estate, I can tell you 9 out of 10 wholesalers will not have any issue with you sending their deals out to your buyers list. If they're smart, they will see this situation as a tremendous asset to them as it is giving their wholesale deals more exposure to potential cash buyers. After all, wholesalers' number one goal is to sell the deal that they spent so much time acquiring.

Essentially, you will be playing the middleman, coordinating showings between your buyer and the wholesaler to go see properties that you have available through your network.

Before offering wholesalers' properties to your buyers, a significant note to consider is the impact of the laws of your state to ensure that you're not required to have a real estate license to offer other wholesalers properties. The laws may even require a marketing agreement signed by the wholesaler to give you permission and transfer equitable interest to you, giving you the right to market that equitable interest.

The next category of people is cash buyers. This area you want to invest a good portion of your time, like 90%, is in building your cash buyers list. Not all cash buyers are wholesale deal cash buyers, but, if you become a knowledgeable professional, you can turn them into wholesale deal cash buyers.

You will find these buyers similarly to how you're find your wholesalers. Some of the people that you will run into at these meetings you will be frequenting often will be cash buyers. When you find them, you are going to let them know that you're a wholesaler. You will tell them that you're starting to build your business and you would like to add them to your cash buyers list to be able to send them deals periodically. You will find any serious buyer very receptive to the idea of receiving more possible deals.

This conversation should be a very easy one to have, so there is no need to be self-conscious about your knowledge in the industry. Again, you will find most of these people to be very forgiving of any lack of decorum when it comes to real estate investing and will usually be very enthusiastic about offering ideas and knowledge to you.

Another place you will find cash buyers will be in public record. You should become very familiar with ways of researching properties in your local area, municipality or city. Nowadays, most areas have all their records online and, in many cases, have interactive maps that allow you to click on different parcels and different properties that have been sold recently to find out the name of the buyer and the parties that were involved in the transaction.

From these records, you should be able to find the mailing addresses of the buyers that purchased the property. The ones you should be looking for are going to be some type of entity, meaning an LLC, CORP or INC. You can then put them on a drip mail campaign every couple weeks, sending them a simple cheap postcard telling them what you do and that you have properties available, as well as giving them your contact information or a place where they can email you their contact information.

The more you build these lists of wholesalers and cash buyers, the more deals you will be able to complete. This process is your first step in the LYNK Real Estate Investing System.

The LYNK way of real estate investing allows you to start making money even before you even know how to write a contract, close a deal, talk with sellers, run comparables or evaluate repairs—you don't need to know any of this! You can learn these things as you are making money. We want you making money now because your money will give you motivation and will start the snowball to ultimate success!

The power of the LYNK Wholesaling System is huge. By eliminating risk, there is no reason for you to fail. There is no way to lose money, you can remove the fear that you don't know enough to start yet. You can no longer use these excuses! The time is now!

The Time to Act is Now!

Chapter 10: Building a Deal Engine

If you truly want to be a successful LYNK Wholesaler, then building a deal engine is a step you cannot skip.

Over the course of this book, you will notice that we emphasize the importance of being a master networker over and over again. The reason why we focus so much on networking goes back to the old saying, "Your network is your net worth." It really is the truth. You should take this saying to heart as you begin your journey into LYNK Real Estate Investing.

If you network correctly, wholesalers are going to be the source of a continuous and overflowing amount of deals. This network of wholesalers is going to allow you to create a non-stop deal engine of incoming wholesale properties ready to be sold that you can present to your network of cash buyers. Because of this, ensure that you never stop actively looking for new wholesalers! They are vital in providing you with fresh deals and, oftentimes, better deals to present to your buyers list.

If you apply all of the tactics and methods on finding wholesalers that we will show you in the following pages, you will, without a doubt, be able to develop a massive deal engine that will be the building blocks of your real estate career and generate profit for years to come. As you gain more experience and continue to use these tactics day in and day out, you will see just how powerful it is to have a massive wholesale deal engine network.

Local REIA's

This is one of the easiest and most cost-effective (meaning free) ways by which you can start to build your network of local wholesalers while also making a name for yourself in the process.

One of the very first things you should do when embarking on your list building is finding out where all of your local real estate investment associations and meetings are held. Find out if there are any sub meetings being held for any niches in your market and start attending every single meeting they have.

If you are able to at this point in your business, I would recommend that you pay for memberships to your local chapters and, if possible, reserve a table where you can be showcased. As their members mingle, you will have the chance to meet many people. Not only will you be able to build a great network compiled of different types of real estate professionals, but you will also likely learn some great things about your local market from the speakers that will be at these meetings.

Remember, don't be shy! If you're new to this whole thing, keep in mind that people go to these meetings specifically to meet new people. In this case, you want to be that new person that they meet at every meeting. So, if possible, introduce yourself to everyone that is attending and give out as many business cards as you can.

Facebook

Facebook is a great place to meet local, like-minded real estate professionals, especially wholesalers. There are dozens of very large wholesaling groups that you can search and become a part of. I recommend you that do join these groups immediately.

Start posting in these groups several times a week and engage in the conversations with questions or dialogue that you see on a day-to-day basis. This will familiarize you with the active members and them with you. Let them know that you're a cash buyer but that you're also a wholesaler and have a massive buyers list of local and international cash buyers looking for properties right now. You can either direct message them or just post your deal specific email address into any comment that is relevant or onto ongoing conversations that may be relevant.

The best way to get the most deals is to leave your email address in the open comment section as it will stay there forever. As new members come into the group, they will likely go back and search previous conversations and your email will be there for them to find.

Forums

Forums are not as popular as they once were, especially since social media has become so popular. However, there are still some big real estate forums out there where you can make some great connections.

To find the best real estate related forums on the Internet, search for as many as you can find and simply join them all. As an active member, you'll be able to see just how engaging the other members are and will help you make a determination as to which ones are most active.

Don't delete any of the other profiles that you've made thus far, though. Keep them all. You should be actively posting anywhere you possibly can, but at least now you'll have an expectation as to what kind of interactions you're going to have on the smaller forums.

As for how to interact with other members, you'll handle those the same way as you do while networking on social media. Keep an eye out for the proper conversations, leave your email address and state your intentions. You can even start a forum topic about wholesaling and see what kind of feedback you receive.

We Buy Houses Websites

This method is perhaps the easiest way to quickly get your first 50 to 100 active buyers and real estate professionals on your list. Simply go to all the major search engines online and search for "we buy houses," "sell my house fast," "need to sell my house" and any other related searches you can think of.

Almost all the sites you will find will be clearly identifiable as belonging to real estate investors and will usually have phone numbers and email addresses right there on the website.

Many of these websites will be wholesalers looking for deals to put under contract. I recommend that you call them before using these email addresses to find out if they are a wholesaler or a buyer so you can categorize them correctly.

Kill two birds with one stone using this method.

CraigsList

Many wholesalers use Craigslist to market their properties. They will post them in the "for sale" section of the website under houses and/or properties.

The great thing about Craigslist is that you have the ability to not only search for the current listing, but also search for the past listing that a wholesaler may have posted. To distinguish a wholesaler from just a typical seller, you'll want to look out for key words and phrases.

Some words and phrases include:

- "Cash Sale"
- "Fixer Upper"
- "Cash Only"
- "No Inspections"
- "Cash or Hard Money Only"
- "Handyman Special"
- "Rehab Potential"

- "Home Needs TLC"
- "Wholesale Deals"

These terms and phrases can identify a wholesaler that is attempting to sell one of their properties because they are using terms and phrases that require the purchaser to buy the home as is and for cash.

Chapter 11: Wholesaler Scripts

Here are a few sample scripts that you can use when contacting wholesalers.

New Wholesaler Phone Contact:

My name is {name}. I'm giving you a call because I see that you guys have wholesale deals and I'd like to be on your buyers list. We are expanding into this area and are looking to build some relationships. Can I text you to the number I called with my info and email address?

Wholesaler Asks:

Question: *"Are you a cash buyer/wholesaler?"*

Answer: *We are cash buyers and we also have a large network of local and international cash buyers looking for deals. So, we are looking to* buy and also possibly joint venture by selling some deals to our buyers.

Question: *"What kind of deals are you looking for?"*

Answer: *We will look at any deal, any price point. Single family, multi family or condo/townhouse.*

Finding out Wholesalers Protocols:

Hey, "Wholesaler," this is {your name}. I have a bunch of buyers that I think would be interested in some of your deals.

I wanted to call you first to see if you would be okay with me marketing your properties to my buyers? Also wanted to see how it would work if I was able to sell a deal for you?

Are you okay with us doing a simple "JV," joint venture agreement, fee if I sell one of your deals to my buyers?

Chapter 12: Building a Massive Buyers List

When used properly, the secrets and hacks you'll learn in this book will make you untold amounts of money throughout your career in LYNK Real Estate, and having a massive buyers list is one incredibly important part.

The importance of having a quality list of "whale" and "baby whale" buyers cannot be expressed enough. Some of these buyers, known as whale buyers, can purchase an unlimited amount of properties from you because they have very deep pockets. Others, the baby whale buyers, will buy 5 to 10 properties a year and will be a consistent source of profit for you as you offload properties to them, year after year.

Having the best buyers list in town will crown you the king of the real estate mountain. If you apply the methods we will show you in the coming pages you'll be well on your way to building your massive buyers list. The biggest fear that many wholesalers face is not being able to sell their deals once they finally get one. Master the art of building your buyers list and you will never experience this fear.

Here are some of the ways that we have used to build one of the best buyers list ever created. They are not listed in order of importance as they can all be extremely effective and are designed to bring in a massive amount of buyers in their own right.

Contractors and Builder

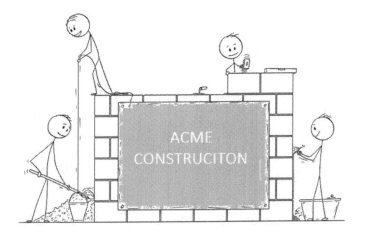

Contractors, builders and construction firms are another great place to find cash buyers. You can usually contact your city or county and get a list of all the licensed contractors in your area. These lists will provide will usually contain some kind of contact information for each business or individual.

You can also search the internet for contractors and builders. Visit their website and contact them. Let them know what you do and ask if they are interested in receiving your discount wholesale properties.

These interactions can also be a great source of potential partnerships. You can ask them if they are willing to partner with you if you find a great deal. Keep a list of all the people that say they are willing to do so and, as you get further along into the business, you'll have a great network of experienced contractors that you can do some rehabs with when you get to that level.

We Buy Houses Websites

This method is perhaps the easiest way to quickly get your first 50 to 100 active buyers and real estate professionals on your list. Simply go to all the major search engines online and search for "we buy houses," "sell my house fast," "need to sell my house" and any other related searches you can think of.

Almost all the sites you will find will be clearly identifiable as belonging to real estate investors. Though most of the sites will have their contact phone number clearly displayed on the webpage, not all will have an email address. Instead, you may see a contact form in place of an actual email address.

The best way to identify whether or not the website or company that you found is run by a cash buyer or a wholesaler is to simply call the phone number and have a quick conversation.

Treat this call just as you would any other interaction with a cash buyer by explaining that you would like to add them to your buyers list.

Social Media/REI Forums

Needless to say, everything is online nowadays. If you are not building your network on all the major social media platforms and REI forums, you have to start ASAP.

Most people tend to only use these platforms for friends, family and pictures of their pets and food. Let's be honest—you don't need to use social media for friends and family. They already know who you are.

If you want to make a lot of money and be a master networker, as you should, you have to use these as a professional platform. You should be using these platforms to build your network with individuals that don't know you. Use them to build your brand as a LYNK Wholesaler—as the only person a buyer would need to go to in order to find a good deal.

Start posting about what you do as a LYNK Wholesaler in all the real estate related groups and forums. You'll find this is a great tool to quickly build your real estate network.

Local REIA's

This is one of the easiest and most cost-effective (meaning free) ways by which you can start to build your network of buyers while making a name for yourself in the process. One of the very first things you should do when embarking on your list building is finding out where all of your local real estate investment associations and meetings are held.

Find out if there are any sub meetings being held for any niches in your market and start attending every single meeting they have. If you are able to at this point in your business, I would recommend that you pay for memberships to your local chapters and, if possible, reserve a table where you can be showcased. As their members mingle, you will have the chance to meet many people.

Not only will you be able to build a great network compiled of different types of real estate professionals, but you will likely learn some great things about your local market from the speakers that will be at these meetings.

Remember don't be shy! If you're new to this whole thing just keep in mind that people go to these meetings specifically to meet new people. You want to be that new person they meet at every meeting. So, if possible, introduce yourself to everyone that's attending and give out as many business cards as you can.

Driving For Dollars

Driving for dollars is usually attributed to finding distressed sellers within properties that look vacant. However, it can also be a very good way to find active rehabbers and landlord buyers in your area. As you drive around, look for properties that are having work done to them and that are vacant. Stop at those properties.

Talk to the workers and give them your business card. Tell them to please contact the owner and have him or her give you a call telling them that you would like to buy their house. This is a surefire way to have the owner call you.

You can also call any property that has a "for rent" sign. This is a great source to add depth to your list and add landlord-buyers.

Call the number on the sign and let the lessor/property owner know that you have rental properties available. Since they have one property for rent, let them know that you thought that they may be interested in seeing other properties that they can rent out. Ask for their contact information and let them know you'll be in touch as soon as you get your next property.

Chapter 13: Buyer Scripts

Here are a few sample scripts you can use for your buyers.

New Buyer Text/Email/Return Call:

Hey, {buyer name}. I see you are asking about {property address}. I will get you some info on that, but I always like to give a quick call first to anyone that we haven't worked with before. Do you have a moment? ---

Great, just wanted to let you know how the process works with us. All of our properties are available to purchase with cash or hard money only. We don't sign contracts that have financing contingencies.

Also, I want to let you know that all inspections must be done prior to us executing a contract. With these types of properties, we usually have limited access and are only able to set one or two appointments to view the house, so you would want to do your full evaluation in one visit to the property.

One last thing, we do offer clear title with no liens or violations unless our email states otherwise, and that's pretty much it... Do you have any questions for me?

I'm going to get you the info on the property you called about and text you my contact info. Thanks!

New Buyer Call In:

Since we haven't had a chance to close a deal together yet, I always like to take a moment to go over a few key points and let you know how it works buying from us, and then answer any questions you may have.

To start:

All the properties you see on our list are "wholesale," and what that means is that they are under contract and we are flipping them to other investors like yourself...

Inspections:

We don't give inspection contingencies on these properties. We can arrange access for you to assess the property condition and repairs needed, but most of the time you will only be able to get inside the property once so you should be ready to make a decision after that.

Upon acceptance of your verbal offer, we will prepare the contract package and send it out to you.

The purchase would need to be cash or hard money, we don't accept traditional bank financing since they don't finance wholesale flip transactions. Other than that, it is pretty straight forward. Do you have any questions?

Chapter 14: Mastering Negotiations

In this chapter, we will go over how to master negotiations. It is our hope that by completely reviewing this material you will have a full understanding about what it takes to persuade an argument or a negotiation in favor of yourself and come out victorious.

If you put these techniques to practice and use them even in your day-to-day life, you'll be surprised by your ability to determine the outcome of any situation you may face.

These tactics and ideas are the result of tens of thousands of phone calls, negotiations, and trial and error. You can rest assured that we have been there and done that, so there's no need for you to go through the same hard fought battles in order to find out what works best. We have done it all for you.

This chapter is designed to bring all the elements together that are needed become a strong negotiator as well as the specific strategies and techniques necessary to maximize every negotiation, phone call, and generated lead at the highest possible level.

Hopefully, you already have an understanding about how vitally important it is to be a good salesperson. If, however, you are new to this, let me take a moment to explain what I mean.

If you've never given thought to the fact that being a good salesperson and having great negotiation skills is vital to your overall success in life, now is the time to train yourself to think this way. It is extremely important for you to understand that having strong and confident sales skill set will be the ultimate determining factor in your eventual success or failure.

The ability to dominate the deal-making process and negotiations of that deal are vital to protecting profits at every level throughout your career. Applying the skills and tactics you will learn here to LYNK Real Estate Systems will surely set your place as the alpha.

It is also important to note that we insist in using all this material with the highest ethical standards and not in a way that would persuade people to do things that would not be in their best interest. These techniques are so persuasive that you must be mindful to use them to affect good at all times.

It's our belief that having powerful sales and persuasion skills are key to creating massive wealth and success for yourself but also being able to influence others that you care about and encourage them in a powerful way to do the same.

The true secret to negotiating is understanding that the whole sales process is the negotiation. If you have an ironclad presentation and process, then you will not even have to negotiate the price in most cases and, if you do, it will be very little.

Understanding this will set you apart from the rest. Negotiating is not just saved for the money aspect of a deal. When you position yourself as a person of authority and can persuade the other party where your position is too logical and compelling to think otherwise, they will have no choice but to give you their money!

In order to be successful at mastering negotiations, you must be committed to some basic entrepreneurial guidelines. These guidelines include the following:

- The drive and determination to constantly learn and grow

- The ability to recognize and quickly take advantage of opportunities that are presented to you

- A burning desire to create wealth and be wealthy

- A commitment to an outstanding work ethic and the ability to deliver results.

I recommend that you go through this material several times and purposely put yourself in an environment where you be pushed to apply this information several times a week in order for it to fully take root in your mind and subconscious.

Negotiation Tactic One: A.B.R.

The old way of closing sales and persuading was thought of as the ABC method, or the Always Be Closing method. In reality, it really should look like ABR method, the Always Building Relationships method.

Once you realize this, closing and confirming deals during the closing process really only becomes about 10% of the equation. You need to be identifying the needs and presenting solutions to those that you have a relationship with.

This doesn't mean that you're going to become friends with every prospect that you meet. What it does mean is that you need to have a friendly relationship with these individuals because you want to establish trust.

Ultimately, you will need their trust if you want to win the sale. The best way to gain someone's trust is through giving them valuable information that is useful and solution-based and giving it to them for free.

Negotiation Tactic Two: Stay on Point

When speaking to a prospective buyer, you must know the beginning and the end of your sales pitch. In order to make the sale, you must be talking on the topic of the sale. If you are trying to sell someone a house, for example, and they begin to discuss a different topic, then you won't be able to make the sale unless you bring the topic back to the house.

The art of negotiating comes in when you're trying to make this sale persuasively and with conversational rhythm. You don't want the prospect to think that you don't care about what they're talking about; however, you need to stay on point as a professional in your field and be the expert that they need to believe you are. Keep the conversation relevant.

Let's say, for example, that you're trying to negotiate the sale of a house. You're discussing the terms with the potential buyer, but they begin speaking about their pets.

Remember, if you're doing your job right, the buyer should feel very comfortable speaking to you, so it's understandable that they would speak about personal events in a friendly manner. However, your job is to swing the conversation back to where you want it.

So, if they are discussing the fact that they just adopted a Labrador, you should take the opportunity to respond with a comment like,

"This is a perfect house for pets," or "that's great; have a look at this yard, your dog is going to love it." This way, you remain personable, yet you still remain in control of the topic of the conversation and keep it on the sale of the home.

Negotiation Tactic Three:
Expertise = Rapport

To negotiate effectively, you must build rapport and gather intelligence effectively. Contrary to popular belief, you do not want to start talking about yourself or asking 100 personal questions of your prospective buyer thinking that will help you build rapport. The most effective way to maximize a negotiation is for your prospect to believe and see that you are an expert and that you want to get them to their goal quickly and professionally.

In order to effectively gather intelligence, you need to talk less and to listen to more. Oftentimes, silence is better than unnecessary conversation. When you do speak, you must be able to identify the key questions to ask the prospective buyer that will be specific to the type of property or item that you're selling at that time, and then let the prospect talk.

The questions you will ask need to be purposeful and ones that will help you understand if what you're selling is a proper fit for your prospect. If you find out through your questions that it's not a good fit for them, you need to end the encounter and find a different product or property for that prospect.

In addition, if you identify that a property is not right for the prospect, let them know. Explain that it's not a good deal for them, and you'll build rapport immediately. This will almost always ensure future sales with that buyer.

Negotiation Tactic Four:
Sell Yourself First

You must be totally convinced in your sale and confident if you want to persuade someone. In order to be confident and convincing, you need to be knowledgeable. Take the time to research, study and learn about what it is you're selling. You need absolute knowledge about what you are presenting to the prospect.

You don't have to get a degree in the field of your product; you just have to have enough knowledge to be able to articulate your opinion properly. You simply must be able to make a valid, factual argument that can accurately explain and represent your product. If you're trying to sell a buyer a house, you need to have all the details. You need to know if there are any issues with the house as well as other pertinent information to support your position.

Remember that the first thing you need to sell is going to be yourself. If you can't sell yourself, then how can you expect to sell someone else?

Always remember, almost everything in life revolves around sales. You're either selling yourself, a product, or a service, or you're being sold a product, service or trust in a person.

Negotiation Tactic Five: Enthusiasm

This section is where you begin to understand the importance of the tone of your voice at different parts of your sales process.

When you're first telling somebody about a house or opportunity, you need to sound excited, confident and enthusiastic, as well as be concise.

Remember that people want to relate to other people, and they do it subconsciously whether they know it or not. So, when you're talking, while at the same time being enthusiastic and confident, your prospect will naturally pick up on these emotions and follow along. This mirroring will add to the momentum of your sales process and bring them further along down the closing line, which will allow you to continue to build on this momentum.

The best way to accomplish this tactic successfully is to start by matching the prospects enthusiasm and tone, then elevating it slowly to bring it to where you want to be during the sale pitch.

When you do this correctly, it's a completely unnoticeable change in the conversation, yet the prospect will be more enthusiastic and also view you as more trustworthy than before.

The change in enthusiasm invokes a primal connection of trust.

Mirror this and it works every time!

Chapter 15: LYNK and Beyond

One thing we know from our collective experience is that having a clear vision and clear expectations in business can be a great driving force for your motivation. Knowing that there is a path forward, another step that can be taken, or a higher achievement that can be completed, will keep you moving in the right direction.

Our LYNK Wholesaling program will stand as a benchmark for your future business by proving to yourself that real estate is accessible to you and can be achieved through dedication and hard work. The true beauty of this progressive system is that it uses all of the inside secrets and tricks of real estate and puts them at the disposal of even the most inexperienced prospective new investor.

Each step of this program, when followed properly, is a building block of trust, confidence, motivation and success. It is designed to keep you interested, intrigued, learning, engaged and dedicated so that, in your mind, there will be no option for failure.

Let me lay out a path so that you can see exactly where LYNK Real Estate Investing can take you. As we discussed in detail, you would start off with LYNK Wholesaling, the art of selling deals for other wholesalers. This section truly is the lowest barrier to entry into real estate investing for anyone. There is no feeling like the pride you will have through consistently and successfully closing deals. LYNK Wholesaling makes this whole process easy. In no time, your friends and family will be asking what you're doing as you start making better decisions and putting money away.

The next step in our system is LYNK Flipping. This part of our course is where we unveil how to start flipping your own wholesale deals to motivated sellers without having to spend a dollar on advertising. Again, our goal in everything we put together for you is to maximize the potential for success and minimize the risk of loss and failure. We do not want you losing money!

This section also relates to wasting money. You can waste money by wasting time, by making mistakes, and by doing the wrong type of advertising. One huge way of wasting money is advertising when you are not prepared to capitalize on quality leads. It is very easy to spend thousands of dollars when trying to get motivated sellers. If you don't know how to properly negotiate, evaluate, and market your wholesale deals to your buyers, you will waste a lot of time and money.

Through LYNK Wholesaling, you will be able to learn all these vital skills and personality traits that will be needed when it's time to risk a little bit in getting your own wholesale deals and learn it risk free.

This is why LYNK Flipping is a must do next step for anyone who wants to become a full time LYNK Real Estate Specialist. This section allows you to progress into actually flipping your own wholesale deals while still learning how to properly negotiate, how to properly advertise, how to prepare and negotiate contracts, and how to close deals.

One thing you would never want to do is start spending money on advertising and marketing to sellers of off-market properties when you don't know how to close a real estate transaction and all the things that it will entail. There are many pitfalls and traps that you can fall into along the way to a closing, and we want to insulate and minimize the possibility that any of these things will derail your momentum.

Sometimes, for instance, you simply "don't know what you don't know," and this lack of knowledge can be very costly when you're spending money to get deals. For example, let's say that you're spending what would likely amount to thousands of dollars in order to get an off-market deal with an ongoing marketing campaign. However, you make a simple mistake that causes that deal not to close. Not only did you lose the advertising dollars that it cost to get that deal in the first place, but you have also lost the profit that you would have gained from closing that transaction.

This is why we have designed the LYNK Wholesaling System to graduate you progressively and incrementally into the lowest risk but highest possible return investment strategies one step after the other. We will show you, in your next step, how to target properties that you know the owners want to sell and how to do that without spending a dollar on advertising.

We have devised a system to build upon the hard work and risk of others who are in the market and finding motivated sellers and show you a way to use these properties as a stepping stone for your LYNK Real Estate business development. Just to drive the point home, everything we teach you is legal, ethical and planned specifically to create an environment in which that seed of entrepreneurship can flourish.

What I'm describing to you here is considered phase one of our LYNK Flipping System. Once you have graduated from this section and have several closed transactions under your belt and some profit in your bank account, you will enter phase two of the system. In this phase, we show you some of the more traditional routes of wholesaling real estate deals, but with a Miami twist.

All of our strategies and systems have been developed through our experience flipping hundreds and hundreds of properties in one of the toughest and most competitive markets in the world—Miami, Florida! If you can master our LYNK Investing System that we've used to grow a wildly successful company here in South Florida, you can dominate your market.

The next link in your chain of successful investing strategies you will learn is the LYNK

Fix-n-Flip System. At this point, you would have already mastered selling other wholesalers deals, completed Phase 1 and 2 of LYNK Flipping and now have a conveyor belt of deals coming your way that are ripe for the picking. Money will no longer be a problem for you and, in fact, you will actually have become an investor, using your money to make money.

This is where you are able to cherry-pick deals that you want to rehab yourself, or rather the team that you will put together to rehab these deals. We will take you through how to minimize potential traps and costly mistakes by starting out with our Lipstick-on-a-Pig strategy that will be your entry point the rehabbing properties.

This is the easiest lowest risk, most cost-effective way to start gaining experience while rehabbing your first batch of properties. We will show you what type of properties to target for this strategy, what makes a good candidate for a bad candidate, and how to accomplish every step of the way.

I will show you what design trends you should target and which ones you should stay away from how to maximize profit and capitalize on the hot Miami market trends, and introduce them to your area to be ahead of the pack. You'll have people fawning and offering above asking price on your properties.

If you can't picture yourself in this position just yet, don't worry. As you go through our system and see how easily all these things can actually be accomplished you can be a master LYNK Wholesale Specialist and fast as your desire and dedication can get you there.

Knowledge is Power!

Chapter 16: The Right People, the Right Questions

As you grow your mindset as an entrepreneur and a real estate investor, you will have to evaluate whom and where you get your advice from.

This may sound harsh, but when it comes to finances, investing, and your future as an investor, you should avoid the advice of your family and friends at all costs. Unless they are in a position in life that you would like to reach yourself, you should avoid their advice. The advice that you get from family and friends will be given with the best of intentions, however, it doesn't mean it is right or that you should use it.

When was the last time they, who so easily gave you advice, invested in themselves? When was the last time that they skipped partying over the weekend in order to take a course that could better their life and advance their financial situation? Sadly, our experience shows the answers to these questions will be almost never. Understanding the reality of the situation will put you in front of the pack, and applying these concepts can bring you out of obscurity and into prosperity. Your goal should be to become the person that they would come to for advice because your success has become so apparent and blatant that they start asking what it is you've done.

This reminds me of something that someone I admire greatly used to tell me: "If you need to fix a pipe under your sink, you don't call the roofer." Simple and understated, yes, but it is very effective if applied correctly. What I mean is, by using this statement as a guideline, you would never ask family or friends if they think real estate is a good idea, or if they approve of you becoming a real estate investor or investing in a course for yourself or furthering your knowledge base. You must understand that, in order to be successful as a real estate investor, you will have to do things that other people, even family and friends, will consider risky, crazy, foolish, or even outright stupid.

What never ceases to amaze me is that the same people that would tell you not to take that course, not to become a real estate investor, not to further your knowledge base, would give you an enthusiastic yes if you were to ask them if you should go to college or go back to college and further your degree, without even asking the cost. They would tell you yes even if they themselves never went to college or had any benefits from it.

Why is that? It's because society has drilled this notion into all of our heads since we were children that going to college is the right thing to do. I would argue that the only benefits anyone would ever receive from going to college would be the accolades awarded if they have chosen a profession that has the ability to make them a millionaire. As mentioned before, some promising careers include an attorney, doctor, engineer, computer scientist, etc...

If you truly want success and a life where money comes easy, a life that you can enjoy full of freedom, you have to surround yourself with the right people that can help get you there!

It is imperative that you seek out the advice of industry leaders. You should reach as far up the chain as your money can buy. Why, you may ask, do I mention spending money? If you look at the ratio of successful industry leaders versus the ordinary Average Joes in this world, it is 10 to 1. The odds of you already knowing someone super successful are slim to none.

So, how do you connect with a successful person in real estate investing that you will be able to learn from and gain experience from? This is why I mention money; anyone who is worth their salt and that has become super successful will not do what they're good at for free.

I know it is counter-intuitive to the psychology of our society that wants to save, conserve, and protect every penny. However, take a look at all the people following that model–that's what we call the lower and middle class. So, in order to ask the right people the right questions in many cases you will need to pay for proximity! You should look at this as a privilege, an obligation, and an ethical duty to your dreams and to your family or future family to do this.

You will never know everything there is to know about real estate–no one does. It doesn't matter what real estate course you take or how great it is; you will always find yourself in a position where there's a new problem that needs to be solved in order to get that deal closed, make that transaction work, or further your business.

This is what we're paying for; proximity is invaluable. What will you do when you have $30,000 or $40,000 on the line to get a deal closed in the next 4 or 5 days and you didn't spend the money and take the time to build that relationship with a mentor? How valuable will that relationship be to you at that point? Do it before you need it and it will save you and make you tons of money.

Having the right players on your team, whether paid for or earned, can make you millions of dollars. Avoiding costly mistakes, saving deals, circumventing problems, and closing hard transactions are what will separate you from the amateurs and make you tons of money. Being able to call and get a quick answer to a tough question can be the difference between making and losing money on a deal.

The quicker you realize this, the better off you will be. If you find the right mentor and the right group to become a part of, what would be a one-time cost to you now could be years and years of questions answered, problems avoided, and deals closed because of those relationships that you invested time and money into in the beginning.

Don't be afraid, step out from your comfort zone and interact with other professionals and find a mentor.

Chapter 17: What's Next?

The information we've provided in this book should give you the jump start you need to start your career as a LYNK Wholesaler.

If you want to learn more tactics, tricks and strategies, we're here to help. We have compiled an A-Z course on every aspect of the LYNK Wholesaling process. We take a deep dive into real estate wholesaling and provide you with a step by step guide on how exactly to succeed.

Simply visit our Real Estate Training Center at

www.LigonU.com

(https://www.ligonu.com/)

BONUS: 5 Keys to Success

As a bonus, here are 5 key components that every aspiring entrepreneur should know and follow to be successful.

Key One:

Invest in Yourself

Successful entrepreneurs invest in their minds and their bodies. They pay for knowledge as often as possible. Acquiring knowledge allows you to accelerate your success by buying experience. Buying experience allows you to buy time, and every successful person knows time is the only thing we can never get back.

Key Two:

Be Confident and Resourceful

Successful entrepreneurs develop confidence in their abilities. Knowledge builds confidence, and being more confident breeds healthy actions and decisions.

When you are confident in your abilities, you tend to be more resourceful with your decision making.

Key Three:

Be Self-Motivated

All successful entrepreneurs understand the importance of being self-motivated. You cannot leave your motivation up to others. Remember that not everything will always go as planned. Accept that fact, adapt and move on.

Understand that the pressure is a privilege.

Key Four:

Be Passionate

Successful entrepreneurs identify their passion points. Ask yourself: what do you feel passionate about? Is it helping others, building a network, or something else? Be passionate about your purpose. Be enthusiastic about your goals, learn to love the journey.

This will, in turn, assist you in being self-motivated.

Key Five:

Be Willing to Risk for Profit

All successful entrepreneurs understand that you must be willing to risk in order to succeed. You must be willing to invest time and money without fully knowing the outcome.

More often than not, there is not instant gratification. Success is a journey. You must be able to travel that journey outside your comfort zone.

Follow these 5 Keys and you will be on your way to a successful life!

Conclusion

We hope that, at the very least, we have opened your eyes to the possibility that a successful career in real estate investing is within your reach. We hope that the steps we have laid out can bring this lifestyle into a reality for you and your family or your future family.

We're passionate about helping others achieve success in their life through real estate. Our LYNK Real Estate Investing System has been developed over many years after completing, as of the time of this book, over 500 real estate transactions in one of the toughest, most competitive, brutal real estate markets in the world, Miami, Florida. Miami is notorious for being an extremely fast paced and Bellwether market in our country and the world. If you dive in and use the successful system that we have developed in this tough market, then you should be able to dominate anywhere you implement these strategies.

By dedicating yourself to achieving your dreams, using real estate as the vehicle to success and the tactics that got us to where we are today, you can go wherever your heart desires. You don't have to do it on your own. We've already made the mistakes and paved the way! Just copy what works, and success will find you right where you are. We wish you unlimited success!

Good Luck!

"Having mentors is a must if you want to succeed. If you want to be a successful person, you have to buy knowledge and mentorships whenever possible and surround yourself with successful people!"

~ The Ligon Brothers ~

About the Authors

David Ligon   Michael Ligon

The Ligon Brothers

The Ligon Brothers are Real Estate Investors, Entrepreneurs, Coaches and Mentors.

They've taken their overwhelming experience in the field of real estate investing and used it to develop the Real Estate Connector Method with the LYNK Wholesaling System.

This ground breaking system allows absolutely anyone to begin a career in real estate investing without any prior experience, without any marketing dollars and, best of all, without any risk in the transactions.

Here are some of The Ligon Brothers achievements:

Created the Millionaires Mastermind Circle - 2020

Launched the MLS Digital Flipping Method™ - 2018

Developed the LYNK™ Real Estate System - 2017

Created LigonU, an online Training Center for Real Estate Investing - 2017

Were Recipients of the "Most Deals of the Year" Award - 2016

Florida's Leading Real Estate Investment Firm - 2005 - - -

Flipped Thousands of Real Estate Transactions - Ongoing

Connect with the Ligon Brothers

Facebook: @LigonBrothers

https://www.facebook.com/LigonBrothers

Instagram: @LigonBrothers

https://www.instagram.com/ligonbrothers

Linked In: @LigonBrothers

https://www.linkedin.com/company/ligonbrothers

Twitter: @LigonBrothers

https://twitter.com/ligonbrothers

Website:

https://www.ligonbrothers.com

Online Training Center:

https://www.ligonu.com/

Made in the USA
Columbia, SC
06 September 2020